We Interrupt This Program

The graphic image on the front cover was inspired by this photograph, taken by Ossie Michelin (Inuit) while he was covering the Elsipogtog First Nation's 2013 struggle against corporate encroachment and oil fracking on their ancestral territories in New Brunswick. After the photo went viral, Michelin noted on his website that it had become "a symbol of Indigenous resistance and the power and grace of Indigenous women." Artist Gregg Deal of the Pyramid Lake Paiute tribe in Nevada created the image featured on the cover, an image used widely by groups supportive of Elsipogtog and the Idle No More movement.
| *Photograph courtesy of Ossie Michelin and APTN National News*

We Interrupt This Program

Indigenous Media Tactics in Canadian Culture

Miranda J. Brady and John M.H. Kelly

UBCPress · Vancouver · Toronto

26 25 24 23 22 21 20 19 18 17   5 4 3 2 1

Printed in Canada on FSC-certified ancient-forest-free paper (100% post-consumer recycled) that is processed chlorine- and acid-free.

Library and Archives Canada Cataloguing in Publication

Brady, Miranda J., author
    We interrupt this program : Indigenous media tactics in Canadian culture / Miranda J. Brady and John M.H. Kelly.

Includes bibliographical references and index.
Issued in print and electronic formats.
ISBN 978-0-7748-3508-4 (hardcover).–ISBN 978-0-7748-3510-7 (PDF).–
ISBN 978-0-7748-3511-4 (EPUB).–ISBN 978-0-7748-3512-1 (Kindle)

    1. Native mass media–Canada. 2. Native peoples in mass media. 3. Native peoples and mass media–Canada. 4. Mass media–Social aspects–Canada. 5. Mass media and culture–Canada. I. Kelly, John M. H., author II. Title.

P94.5.I532C22 2017   302.23089'97071   C2017-904960-7
                                                     C2017-904961-5

Canadä

UBC Press gratefully acknowledges the financial support for our publishing program of the Government of Canada (through the Canada Book Fund), the Canada Council for the Arts, and the British Columbia Arts Council.

Printed and bound in Canada by Friesens

Set in ITC Giovanni Std and Univers Lt Std by Marquis Interscript
Copy editor: Jillian Shoichet
Proofreader: Caitlin Gordon-Walker
Indexer: Margaret de Boer
Cover designer: Jessica Sullivan

UBC Press
The University of British Columbia
2029 West Mall
Vancouver, BC V6T 1Z2
www.ubcpress.ca

For Chris and Darlene

Contents

Preface

This book evolved out of our long-standing interest in Indigenous voices of resistance to colonial paradigms, and how Indigenous people actively challenge the limiting identities imposed upon them by the state and popular media. We ask how Indigenous actors intervene in established institutions through media tactics to disrupt the typical flows of image and discourse found in popular culture. As we discuss, institutions can be negotiated and subverted even when they were not originally designed to serve the best interests of Indigenous people.

For Indigenous critics debating the efficacy of established institutions, the stakes are very high. As Indigenous people live the effects of colonization, they are concerned with the ways in which their participation in institutions may inadvertently disadvantage their communities. They are also in a race against time to empower disillusioned young people. According to a Health Canada study published in 2015, the suicide rate of First Nations youth is five to six times higher than that of non-Indigenous youth, with Inuit youth suicide rates among the highest in the world. The legacies of colonial violence continue to plague Indigenous people, and many see both government and privately funded institutions as instrumental in this process, including laws and policies that work to dispossess Indigenous people of their lands and self-determining authority, at times resulting in their displacement and the removal of children from their communities. Too many Indigenous people suffer racism, inadequate government support, disproportionate policing and incarceration, and poverty. They are victims of violence at abhorrent rates. Indigenous women are especially vulnerable with regards to their safety and security. Yet despite the oppressive circumstances in which they find themselves, Indigenous people routinely perform creative expressions of resistance and resurgence using the very apparatuses originally designed to erase them. We honour and explore the nuances of those tactics in this book.

We come to research and write this book from very different perspectives. While Miranda J. Brady has been studying Indigenous identity construction in her academic work for fifteen years, she is a non-Indigenous settler from northern California. John M.H. Kelly is a Skidegate Haida, Eagle Moiety, of the Haida Nation of British Columbia. We further explain our subject positions and our relationship to this work and Indigenous communities in the book's introduction. We believe our individual strengths and experiences complement each other and bring a unique perspective to our research. At the same time, the book reflects not only the complementary aspects of our differing experiences but also the ways in which our perspectives have been put in tension through our collaboration.

We hope we have treated the Indigenous actors described in this book with the dignity and respect they deserve. We hope we have appropriately conveyed their strength and the vital importance of their efforts. We remain at a historical conjuncture where Indigenous lives are always in a struggle against the imperatives of settler society, and we hope our research provides new insights into how media tactics can incite social and political change. As we write, Indigenous activists and allies to the south in the Dakotas are fighting for their Mother Earth, for their lives and our lives. To those and other activists, artists, teachers, elders, community leaders, and survivors who continue the struggle, we say *Haawa* (thank you).

Acknowledgments

There are so many people to whom we owe our gratitude for making this book possible. We would like to start by thanking the participants who generously gifted us with their time, insights, and stories, including Shane Belcourt, Nanobah Becker, Terril Calder, Dana Claxton, Duncan McCue, Kent Monkman, Ry Moran, Alanis Obomsawin, Murray Sinclair, Jason Ryle, and the residential school survivors giving public statements at the TRC's 2013 national event in Montreal. We would also like to express our sincere appreciation to UBC Press and our editor, Darcy Cullen, for her encouragement and confidence in us. She solicited insightful feedback from three anonymous reviewers, which contributed immensely to the development of the book. We thank the reviewers for their detailed comments and prompts for further inquiry. We would like to thank the Social Sciences and Humanities Research Council of Canada for its financial support of this project. Our research assistants were also instrumental during various stages; thanks to Derek Antoine, Emily Hiltz, Lindsay Lachance, Martha Troian, Tamalik McGrath, Pitseolak Pfeifer, and Anna Hoque.

I, Miranda, would like to thank my family, who have been a central part of this project. My partner, Chris Russill, provided intellectual and moral guidance throughout the process, as he always does. We have engaged in more conversations about our respective work than I can count, and he never fails to nourish my thinking and motivate me. My daughter and son, Maya and Ewan, have been incredibly understanding about my divided attention over several years' time. As they grow, I know they will understand the importance of their relationships with place and community, including the

Algonquin people on whose territories we now live, love, and learn. I want to thank my parents, Bonnie and Mike Brady, for their support of my scholarly pursuits throughout the years and their unconditional love; the latter is a precious gift indeed. My mother-in-law, the unflappable Sandy Russill, has also been exceptionally helpful, including the many hours of care and love she devoted to my children while I was away researching and presenting work.

My colleagues, friends, and mentors have been amazingly supportive, and my many conversations with them contributed to the thinking reflected in this book. I would like to acknowledge Salma Monani, Michel Hogue, Debra Merskin, Shoshana Magnet, Pavel Shlossberg, Jeremy Packer, Matt McAllister, Sarah Sharma, Michael Orsini, Melissa Aronczyk, Ira Wagman, Karim Karim, Josh Greenberg, Sheryl Hamilton, Eileen Saunders, Kirsten Kozalanka, David Dean, Carol Payne, Ruth Phillips, and John Sanchez. Anna Hoefnagels, Kahente Horn-Miller, Martha Attridge-Bufton, Sandra Dyck, Brenda Vellino, Jennifer Henderson, and Eva Mackey and our colleagues in Carleton's Centre for Indigenous Research, Culture, Language, and Education (CIRCLE) have also played an important role in informing my intellectual and community-based work. I would also like to acknowledge my students at Carleton University, as we have had many wonderful conversations over the years related to this book, which undoubtedly shaped and inspired my thinking. Finally, I would like to thank my colleague and friend John Medicine Horse Kelly. I have learned so much from seeing how he cares for his communities and treats others, always with kindness and respect.

I, John, would like to thank all the wonderful supporters and contributors that Miranda has already mentioned. In addition, I am forever thankful for my compassionate and talented wife, Darlene Gilson, for her encouragement and patience as we worked on this book. Thank you to all my Haida relatives, who have inspired me. They are too numerous to name one by one. I must, however, especially thank from my heart our beloved Haida matriarch, my cousin Pearle Pearson, and her children and grandchildren, who tirelessly advocate for the value of our language and culture. Thank you to Pearle's sister, cousin Rose, and Rose's husband, Tim. Thank you to Chief Skidegate, Clarence Dempsey Collinson, and his wife, Irene. Thank you to all their children and grandchildren. Thank you to Russ Jones, our clan chief.

The examples set by my grandparents, the Reverend Minister Dr. Peter Reginald Kelly and Gertrude Russ Kelly, taught me that truth and authority do not require a loud voice. Also, I will forever remember with a smile in my heart the lessons and love of our Haida values that I have learned from Horace Lloyd George Kelly (Uncle Jordy), Uncle T. Reginald Kelly, my Aunt Selma, and cousins Kristely Kelly and Isabel Brillon.

At Carleton University, Miranda's acknowledgments have covered my list well, too. Among others are Allan J. and Rae Ryan. My guest lectures in Allan's inspiring Indigenous topics class have been a highlight for me every year for the past fourteen years. I also thank and appreciate those who contributed to the thinking and ethics in the book: Rodney Nelson, Sheila Grantham, Pitseolak Pfeifer, Katherine Graham, and Michele Moffat. I joyfully and deeply acknowledge Elaine Keillor, my dear friend, who was recently awarded the Order of Canada. Her long-time heartfelt work with Indigenous people sets an example among the finest of our allies.

I will always honour my co-author and friend Miranda Brady. Miranda and I could easily continue our acknowledgments for nearly the length of this book and not exhaust the list of the many, many people who have inspired us over the years.

Thank you to every one of you.

statements about the forced removal of Indigenous children from their homes and communities and the systematic abuses they faced in the residential school system. We highlight the courage of residential school survivors as they made their statements and of TRC leaders who attempted to bring their stories to the fore through a highly mediated testimonial process. At the same time, we draw attention to the omission of some Indigenous experiences from the commission's process. Ultimately, we contend that the media practices of the TRC shaped and guided testimonials but left room for resistance to and alternative uses of the process. We also explore possibilities for the TRC's National Centre for Truth and Reconciliation, which will house thousands of digitized survivor testimonials and related documents for a wide Canadian public.

We then describe the Inuk leaders of Nunavut's struggle to gain more control over the context and ways in which Inuit survivor testimonials were to be conducted by the commission. Through productions posted on the IsumaTV media portal, Inuit leaders such as Zacharias Kunuk and Peter Irniq illustrated the importance of including distinct Inuit experiences in the TRC in their own communities and languages. These and other efforts eventually resulted in the formation of the TRC's Inuit sub-commission. Thus, in the process of creating an archive of Inuit survivor testimonial videos, Inuit leaders intervened in the shaping of public memory. The archive is a political, ontological apparatus, a means of asserting Inuit inclusion in the TRC process and the national residential school archive, while at the same time reflecting the Inuit refusal to be conflated with other Indigenous people through the TRC process. The archive and its creation illustrate the distinct experiences of Inuit people, the conditions that shape Inuit historical narratives, and a drive for cultural sovereignty. While colonizers have used archives as mechanisms to mediate, surveil, and control

Indigenous people, and to reproduce and maintain status quo power relations, the IsumaTV project illustrates how archives have also been mobilized to present culturally specific assertions of truth.

Next, we turn to the complex relationship between Indigenous peoples and the popular media, from early photography and painting to film and television, and how such media are natural tools and sites of contestation. There is a close, historical relationship between the proliferation of Indigenous identity constructs; expansionist and nation-building imperatives; and the development of photographs, motion picture, and film. Reductive Indigenous discourses and imagery have circulated widely over the past two centuries through the practices and forms of popular media. We review some of the most common stereotypes in popular media and Hollywood films and argue that such signifiers say more about the imagination of the larger cultures producing and viewing them than they do about Indigenous people themselves. At the same time, we propose a new cultural approach to media studies that considers the particular connotations of Indigenous media practices. Many Indigenous artists and thinkers use the existing media repertoire subversively. We discuss redfacing and remediation in art institutions as popular media tactics employed by Indigenous artists (such as Kent Monkman, Jackson 2bears, and Dana Claxton) in order to turn mainstream media texts and practices on their heads and to shed light on Indigenous erasures. Through their installations in art institutions, their live performances, and their online presence, these artists recontextualize popular visual cues (for example, the vanishing Indian and Indian head iconography) and challenge the assumptions that underpin them.

We then explore the imagineNATIVE Film + Media Arts Festival as an intervention into the film industry, fostering

Indigenous filmmakers in a harshly competitive environment. The original intention of the festival to support Indigenous filmmakers is reflected in its broad, artist-centred treatment of what constitutes Indigenous media. The festival encourages works and filmmakers who refuse filmmaking conventions and those who fully exploit them. By providing support and prioritizing the filmmaker's self-identification rather than abiding by a strict definition of Indigenous aesthetics, the festival provides unique opportunities for Indigenous filmmakers to grow and develop their works. This encourages the proliferation of Indigenous perspectives in film and creative experimentation with genres, forms, and themes, as illustrated through the work of Jeff Barnaby, Terril Calder, and Shane Belcourt, who have all been active in imagineNATIVE over the years.

Finally, we consider some of the most common shortcomings of mainstream news coverage of Indigenous affairs, and the ways in which Indigenous public figures – particularly Anishinaabe reporter Duncan McCue – actively work to intervene in them. McCue works within the confines of mainstream reporting in his position at the CBC, emphasizing the importance of stories and modes of storytelling that are relevant to and appropriate for Indigenous communities. As a journalist for CBC-TV British Columbia and a journalism educator at the University of British Columbia, McCue talks of the importance of training the next generation of news professionals to cover Indigenous affairs with awareness, respect, and relationality. Using our conversation with McCue as a starting point, we discuss the structural limitations of mainstream news media and its ethnocentric reporting with regards to Indigenous issues, as well as the historical distrust with which many Indigenous people view reporters. McCue leaves us on an optimistic note, however, and models another type of journalism, actively involving himself in training Indigenous and non-Indigenous news professionals so that they are better equipped to approach Indigenous issues and communities in a thoughtful and respectful manner.

Media Practices and Subversions

Survivor Testimonials in the Truth and Reconciliation Commission

> This is where it all happened ... hideous things happened ...
> I didn't know nothing about anger. I didn't know nothing about
> hatred. I didn't know nothing about bitterness. But this is where
> I experienced everything ... when I attended that school.
>
> – Mary Shecapio Blacksmith, Montreal, April 2013

In an April 2013 national event in Montreal at the Queen Elizabeth Hotel, Mary Shecapio Blacksmith testified to Canada's Truth and Reconciliation Commission (TRC).[1] Blacksmith was one of 150,000 First Nations, Inuit, and Métis people who as children attended the government-mandated, church-run schools created to assimilate Indigenous children into the larger culture. Blacksmith disclosed her painful experiences of being taken from her parents when she was seven years old, being raped by a priest, and being subjected to harsh corporal punishments for speaking her native Cree language. Blacksmith referred to a clergyman notorious for molesting young girls: "We used to go to church. He would be standing up there, looking for his victims. And I was one of them." She discussed her subsequent struggles with alcohol, drugs, and anger management, and suggested that "there will be no justice if we don't share our stories ... It's like a way out."

Despite the sensitive nature of Blacksmith's testimonial, the sharing circle where she gave her statement was a public and highly mediated affair. The hotel salon in which she spoke was packed with approximately one hundred onlookers, including news reporters typing hurriedly on laptops and academics pointing voice recorders at the speakers and feverishly taking field notes. The audience also included Indigenous attendees, other residential school survivors, and interested members of the public. Camera technicians weaved in and out of the audience with hand-held devices and rolled around larger equipment on wheels. During Blacksmith's talk, five cameras slowly orbited around the circle as their operators attempted to capture the best angle. Statements gathered during the course of the event were streamed live through the TRC's website and will eventually become part of the commission's digital record in its National Centre for Truth and Reconciliation (NCTR). This will lead to a number of possible audiences, meanings, and remediations.[2] The TRC's archive constitutes an important amendment to national history: for more than a century, officials had largely omitted residential schools from Canadian public discourse. Though public discussion is long overdue, we suggest that public mediation of survivor testimonials has deeper implications.

The TRC has recorded testimonials to create "as complete an historical record as possible of the IRS [Indian Residential Schools] system and legacy," which is prescribed by the commission's mandate.[3] This chapter explores the media practices of the TRC in its public statement-gathering process, the coaching that officials provided to speakers for live-audience statements, and the possible afterlife of the testimonial via its remediation in the TRC's NCTR. We include observations of the public statement-gathering process at the April 2013 national event in Montreal, examples from TRC documents and testimonials posted online, and interviews with TRC representatives.

As we argue, mediation did not just capture the testimonial; it was both central to it and constitutive of it. In other words, mediation of TRC testimonials created models for subsequent testimonials. By extension, we suggest the audience affects what happens in testimonials, whether the audience is immediate or an audience "in potentia," made possible through mediation.[4] We suggest that the TRC encouraged particular survivor narratives over others, as it signalled to speakers that they should anticipate the norms and uses of various media forms and narrative guidelines. However, a layer of meta-narrative common in TRC statements suggests resistance to and repurposing of the mediated testimonial form, particularly when we consider the nuances of Indigenous peoples' testimonials against the backdrop of their traditions of cultural knowledge transmission.

The Residential School System and the TRC

The Truth and Reconciliation Commission was established in 2008 as part of the Indian Residential Schools Settlement Agreement among former students, the Government of Canada, and the churches that ran residential schools. It was the largest class action settlement in Canadian history. The residential schools were open from the 1870s; the last federally run Canadian school was closed in 1996. These schools were designed to assimilate Indigenous people into the larger culture and to strip children of their cultural markings by forbidding Indigenous dress, language, and rituals. Survivor Rose Wawakie was born to a traditional family in the bush near Rapid Lake, Quebec, and taken to residential school at the age of six. She stated, "They really do a number on you and your mind. I used to hate myself. I never wanted to be Anishinaabe by the time they got through with me. I wanted to be white."

According to the TRC, more than 150,000 First Nations, Inuit, and Métis children were confined in the schools, often without the consent of their parents. Many suffered physical, psychological, and sexual abuses, and thousands died.[5] Upon returning to their homes years later, survivors reported the hardships they continued to face. Many could no longer communicate with their families in their native tongue or fit in culturally. Often, family members had died in the students' absence.[6] In addition, Indigenous communities have reported intergenerational damage caused by the system. The residential school legacy produced ongoing dysfunction and poverty within Native communities, including mental health issues, family relations problems and estrangement, alcohol and drug addictions, and domestic abuse.[7] Intergenerational survivors provided testimonials to the TRC on the impacts the schools have had on their families and lives. Several survivors at the Montreal event commented that because they were raised in cold, institutional settings, they did not develop the parental skills to connect emotionally with their own children and they perpetuated the violence they learned in the schools.

It should be noted that not all residential school experiences were the same. A number of former students have reported some positive memories, for example, about the friends they made or the pan-Indigenous identities fostered in residential schools.[8] However, TRC testimonials in Canada most frequently centre on traumatic memories.[9]

Until the end of its mandate in 2015, the TRC aimed to "learn the truth about what happened in the residential schools," and to prepare "as complete an historical record as possible of the IRS system and legacy" in order to "inform all Canadians about what happened in the schools."[10] Once finished, this record of survivor testimonials and other relevant documents will be archived and accessible to the public in the NCTR. However, a number of controversies plagued the commission, and it struggled to meet its obligations.[11] For example, the TRC's original board of commissioners resigned after only a year, citing an inability to work together. The Canadian government and the TRC also failed to cooperate in fulfilling the TRC's mandate related to the retrieval of millions of relevant documents from Library and Archives Canada.[12] The Canadian auditor general detailed the situation in an April 2013 report (discussed further below).[13] The TRC's own chair, Justice Murray Sinclair, pointed out in a personal communication some of the commission's limitations:

> I wish I had a couple of hundred million dollars more. I wish I had another lifetime to finish all of this. So it has been a lot of work to try to do this in five years. At the end of the day, we're not going to have it all done as perfectly as it should be done. We are going to have it done as perfectly as we can do it, in the time and with the resources that we've got.

Since it was formed, the commission has also been the subject of a number of critiques from activists, academics, and survivors themselves. Scholars Jennifer Henderson and Pauline Wakeham argue that the TRC and the idea of reconciliation erase a colonial history through a culture of redress.[14] They suggest that the continuing inequalities faced by Indigenous peoples are obscured through visible, short-term gestures such as former prime minister Stephen Harper's 2008 apology to residential school survivors and the formation of the delimited, short-term TRC. According to Henderson and Wakeham, the TRC operated under a misguided "teleological drive" and promoted an idea of reconciliation that worked to conceal the scars of colonization.[15] The idea that the deep-seated problems of colonization and residential schools could be addressed within the five-year span of the TRC (extended to six) was absurd to those who saw the TRC as an effort to placate critics of colonialism and obscure its ongoing effects,[16] such as land dispossession.[17] Similarly, anthropologist and legal scholar Ronald Niezen suggests in *Truth and Indignation: Canada's Truth and Reconciliation Commission on Indian Residential Schools* that the juridical apparatus out of which the TRC emerged oriented all its activities around legal "remedy" of harms done. He argues, "Everything that we associate with this Truth and Reconciliation Commission ... including the ritual, the kinds of emotion publicly expressed, and the form and dominant narratives of testimony – is set within the wider context of this remedial challenge and the solutions found for it."[18] One problem with the legal underpinnings of the class action settlement was the assumption that "harm" was contained and endemic to the schools rather than an inherent feature of settler colonialism and was therefore addressed through monetary award.[19] Moreover, as Niezen suggests, there was a "structural contradiction" in the residential schools claims procedure (the Independent Assessment Process, or IAP) related to residential schools, which ostensibly shaped TRC testimonials. Because the burden of proof was placed on the survivor in the form of testimonial, the process "has disadvantaged some of those who were the most distressed, those who suffered lifelong mental illness, with all the attendant symptoms of trauma such as trouble remembering and acute anxiety when faced with the challenge of recalling traumatic events."[20] Moreover, as witnessed in Montreal, some struggled to locate the required documentation of their enrollment at residential schools, as records had been destroyed, or the records that existed were deemed inadequate by the IAP or Common Experience process.

Another critique has been that the commission's mandate was explicit in stating that its purpose was not to provide names or bring legal action against offenders who molested or harmed Indigenous children.[21] The separate reparations and juridical processes resulting from the settlement agreement included common-experience claims and the IAP. Privacy laws dictated that all identifying information about accused offenders be stricken from TRC testimonials in their final form, and those giving public testimonials were discouraged from disclosing the names of those who assaulted them. Moreover, former students may have been dissuaded from giving public testimonials given the tension resulting from lateral (student on student) abuse in residential schools.[22] The TRC had no juridical power, and its recommendations to the government of Canada were advisory and carried no legal weight.[23]

Critics have maintained a healthy skepticism of Canada's attempts to contain the evidence of such a damnable history in a neat, documented, and archived package. As the onus was placed on Indigenous people to self-manage their pain, Canadians participated in "media witnessing"[24] from a safe and comfortable distance. In Michel Foucault's terms, these sorts of practices help to manage potential dissent or unpredictable effects at a distance.[25] Along these lines, the TRC not only anticipated emotive disclosures; it encouraged manageable affect. By placing survivors in a "field of documentation,"[26] the TRC helped constitute an archive and corresponding system of knowledge about residential schools by promoting certain kinds of disclosure.

We must also consider, however, how testimonials were situated within Indigenous cultural contexts, how they reflected meaningful traditions, and how they were productive for participants. Despite the TRC's limitations, thousands of survivors provided testimonials, with many possible reasons for doing so. In our April 2013 interview, TRC commissioner Justice Murray Sinclair suggested that the TRC had taken about five thousand statements at TRC events. At the time of the TRC's closing in 2015, the NCTR estimated it would eventually house nearly seven thousand video statements from survivors and intergenerational survivors, along with millions of documents provided by government offices and church-es.[27] Those who testified in Montreal in 2013 often expressed appreciation to listeners for hearing their stories. A witness or camera offers an audience, and the process of talking about traumatic events may provide some degree of comfort or emotional release. Victims of traumatic events may wait in anticipation to tell their stories to a sympathetic ear, or what has been described as an "affective community," whether em-bodied, remote, or "in potentia."[28] Critics argue that initia-tives such as the TRC might obscure ongoing injustices, but the TRC held a broader productivity that could not be re-duced to a symbolic gesture. TRC representatives travelled to Indigenous communities, and speakers and audiences were active and passionate participants in TRC activities.

Statement Gathering: Guiding the Process

TRC representatives collected public and private statements in a number of ways. These included community hearings across Canada as well as at larger-scale national events, which tend-ed to be located in urban hubs. During the April 2013 four-day national event in the Fairmont Queen Elizabeth Hotel in Montreal, public testimonials played a key role in the pro-gram, including several sharing circles with the TRC's Survivor Committee, an advisory board consisting of former residen-tial school students. TRC commissioners Justice Murray Sinclair, Chief Wilton Littlechild, and Marie Wilson hosted six sharing panels, which attracted large audiences. The pan-els sometimes included statements from higher-profile sur-vivors, such as Member of Parliament Romeo Saganash, who testified at the national event in Montreal about the death of his brother in a residential school.

Statements given in the commissioners' sharing panels have been streamed live and podcast through the online live video platform livestream.com. The audience looked on while those giving testimonials sat or stood facing the

"the last of his kind" trope as Tonto is depicted as the only survivor of his massacred village.[2]

Contemporary acts of redfacing, including those of Williams and Depp, are culturally complicated and follow a long history of Indigenous objectification and erasure in the American and Canadian public imagination while they work to conceal the continuing legacies of colonial violence.[3] However, the proliferation of Indigenous imagery over the past two centuries has provided a rich archive from which Indigenous artists draw to problematize constructions of Indigenous identity and the omissions they facilitate. Indigenous artists open up dialogue with media texts, forms, and practices by reframing and recontextualizing these constructions through a tactic we describe as remediation.[4]

For example, musical artists A Tribe Called Red screen remixed Indigenous imagery from popular culture in their live performances. Like artist Jackson 2bears, discussed below, A Tribe Called Red appeals to young audiences through hip hop sounds and aesthetics. The band's remediations not only reveal the ridiculous or false nature of Indigenous stereotypes but also illustrate the logic by which they function and may even be empowering.[5] Seeing the many images of "Hollywood Indians" edited and playing together on a loop in A Tribe Called Red performances provides a reference for viewers, one that might not have the same potency if the pervasive images were not played one after the other. The group illustrates that, despite popular imagery, Indigenous people and cultures are neither cemented in the past nor destined for extinction, but alive and thriving in contemporary contexts.

As we discuss in the next section, Indigenous identity has a unique relationship with mediation because colonization happened synchronously with the development of a number of media technologies, including photography and motion pictures. As a result, Indigenous imagery proliferated widely with western expansion and settlement in North America and remains a central part of its imaginary.[6] In particular, Indigenous disappearance, violence, and pacification were popular themes throughout the nineteenth century and the early twentieth[7] and continue in contemporary depictions, such as in the case of the vanishing Indian trope. In the fight against assumptions that Indigenous people are extinct or destined for extinction, remediation is a tactic used to assert Indigenous presence, often with the "vital irony" characteristic of what Anishinaabe writer and scholar Gerald Vizenor calls survivance, or "survival plus resistance."[8]

Remediation is a term applied to media studies by scholars Jay David Bolter and Richard Grusin in their seminal book *Remediation: Understanding New Media*. The idea, connoting a return to or correction, is defined by Bolter and Grusin as "the formal logic by which new media refashion prior media forms."[9] They suggest that "media are continually commenting on, reproducing, and replacing each other."[10] We expand Bolter and Grusin's idea of remediation by exploring the ways in which it is situated against a long cultural and historical backdrop particular to Indigenous experiences.[11] We suggest Indigenous remediation is meaningful in particular ways and explore the cultural subtleties articulated through the media practice.

First, we discuss the colonial relationship between Indigenous people and mediation in Canadian and American histories. We then highlight the work of artists Kent Monkman, Jackson 2bears, and Dana Claxton to demonstrate the diversity of remediation and redfacing as popular media practices with particular connotations in Indigenous artistic expression. We look at how the practice of remediation extends across media platforms that both fit within the confines of art institutions and transcend the gallery walls through new media and live performance. These artists demonstrate the diversity of remediation as a cultural practice, from new takes on old canonical paintings, to hip hop–inspired critiques of the nation gone viral, to single-channel gallery installations and live performances that employ and subvert redfacing. While all three find ways of appealing to wide Indigenous audiences, 2bears and Claxton especially include aesthetic and aural cues that are specific to their cultures (Lakota [Sioux] and Kanien'kehaka [Mohawk], respectively). Similarly, all three artists address in different ways the Indigenous experiences of violence and dispossession.

Indigenous Identity and Mediation: The "Hollywood Indian"

The development of photography and motion pictures at the height of colonizing projects and westward settlement in North America throughout the late nineteenth and early twentieth centuries meant that these technologies had a special relationship with Indigenous people. Common stereotypes in paintings, films, photographs, motion pictures, and novels depicted Indigenous people as uncivilized, non-technological, wise, and mystical.[12] The noble savage and the ignoble savage have remained some of the most persistent identity constructs throughout the years. The noble savage embodies positive attributes, for example, as a friend of the white man, while the ignoble savage is the counterpart of the noble savage, the blood-thirsty "Indian on the warpath."[13] The study of popular, essentialized signifiers of Indigeneity tells us much more about their creators and audiences than about Indigenous people themselves.

Painting, photography, and film shared close ties with the development of anthropology and scientific discourse in the mid-nineteenth century, and scientists employed them to gather supposedly documentary data.[14] Their salvaging impulses reflected sentiments of imperialist nostalgia, a term cultural anthropologist Renato Rosaldo used to describe the lamentation of colonizers over the disappearance of cultures and peoples they have intentionally worked to eradicate.[15]

Filmmaker Edward Curtis used his camera with the same salvaging imperatives in order to capture the iconographic vanishing Indian throughout the late nineteenth and early twentieth centuries. Curtis carefully controlled and edited the images to depict Indigenous peoples in a pre-contact manner, removing Western technologies such as clocks from his photographs and dressing his subjects in wigs and costumes.[16] Curtis's subjects often look downtrodden as they gaze into an uncertain future, as though they know their time is limited and their extinction inevitable. Similarly, in his 1914 film *In the Land of the Head Hunters* (re-released in the 1970s as *In the Land of the War Canoes*), Curtis places Indigenous people in a pre-contact, fictional drama. The film features Kwakwaka'wakw (Kwakiutl) people from the Northwest Coast of British Columbia and Vancouver Island, and includes the alleged Kwakwaka'wakw practice of head-hunting, locking the subjects of this film into a historical and exotic context. As with other early films (such as Thomas Edison's 1894 *Sioux Ghost Dance*), Curtis intentionally portrays traditional activities and rituals that had been outlawed, including the potlatch ceremony (banned in 1844 by the Canadian government), as a means of salvaging.[17]

Similarly, when Robert Flaherty shot *Nanook of the North* in Hudson Bay between 1919 and 1920, he attempted to maintain perceived authenticity by requiring his Inuit actors to dress only in traditional (rather than Western) clothing. Flaherty was influenced by early ethnography, or "the description of cultures, primarily by participant observers from other cultures."[18] The influence of his Indigenous actors, along with the film's location, led reviewers to praise the film's "realism," which of course was contrived. However, as media studies scholar Valerie Alia notes in *Un/Covering the North,* the dichotomy between documentary and fiction in critiques of *Nanook of the North* are problematic as "the production of ethnographic texts is widely acknowledged to be subjective and narrative."[19] Flaherty's films, like other documentary and anthropological texts, privilege an outsider perspective for a mostly non-Indigenous audience.

Perhaps some of the most problematic scenes in *Nanook of the North* place Inuit actors in awkward juxtaposition with Western technologies. The famous scene where a delighted and curious Nanook listens to a gramophone for the first time and attempts to take a bite out of a record is one of these notable instances. Implicit in this scene is the idea that Western technology is superior and that Indigenous people are somehow outside of this technology. As Native American literature scholar Michelle Raheja points out, Allakari-allak, the Inuk actor playing Nanook, was likely familiar with this technology but performed these acts for effect, in essence pulling one over on the audience by pretending to be amazed at the wonders of Western technology.[20] In the process, he was "redfacing," or "playing Indian," in a way that would resonate with his non-Native audience, as the film was created for popular distribution.[21] Nanook as a character is the archetypal noble savage, or friend of the white man.[22]

The concept of survivance, or survival with dignity,[23] is useful for understanding the kind of agency employed by Indigenous actors, including Allakariallak. In the face of impoverished circumstances and a lack of opportunity, many Indigenous actors perhaps saw acting careers as a means of survival.[24] However, as media studies author and scholar Marian Bredin points out, neither economic disadvantage nor lack of control over production explain entirely the participation of Indigenous actors in co-constructing their identities for non-Indigenous audiences. Regardless of the stereotypical roles they often played, Indigenous actors sometimes approached their work with a nod and a wink to knowing audiences who recognized they were merely performing.[25] However, many majority audiences likely perceived Indigenous people who were playing Indian as authentic.

Michelle Raheja and Dakota historian Philip Deloria point to counter-examples in which American Indian directors such as James Young Deer and actors such as Princess Red Wing (Lillian St. Cry), exercised a high degree of agency in guiding filmic productions in the early twentieth century.[26] However, these examples reflect a brief moment in film history, prior to the entrenchment of the Hollywood studio system, after which roles for American Indian actors became much more limited and stereotypical, and it was more difficult for independent filmmakers to enter into the market.

In *Indians in Unexpected Places*, Deloria points out that when the large studio system took hold in the 1920s, it fell out of fashion in Hollywood to hire Indigenous actors to play lead roles in films. It became increasingly difficult for Indigenous people to find work outside of bit parts where they fought and killed white people and were killed en masse themselves. In films from the 1930s to the 1970s, for example, John Wayne often played the archetypal patriot who fought anything and anyone who was a threat to the American way – namely, the ignoble "Indian on the warpath." At the same time, white actors were hired to play Indigenous people in lead roles, in which they spoke in stylized monosyllables to signify their Indian-ness.[27]

While the noble savage and the ignoble savage are most often masculine characters, female archetypes are similarly reductive, and often reflect shifting Euro-American values of morality.[28] S. Elizabeth Bird argues that the most popular depictions of American Indian women over the past 150 years have been the Indian princess or maiden who is uncontrollably drawn to the white man, and the promiscuous squaw who will submit readily to her lusty desires.[29] In *Killing the Indian Maiden*, Indigenous film scholar M. Elise Marubbio identifies this character as the "sexualized maiden" popular in 1940s films, who exhibited these characteristics: "beauty, mixed-blood heritage, out-of-control sexuality, marginalization in white society, and deadliness to men," which "surface in the form of a pinup girl figure."[30] She suggests these characteristics extend into later decades in modified form, changing with the political climate.

These depictions did not reflect the experiences of actual Indigenous people. For example, among the Lakota of the Plains, strict moral codes were the norm. Young women were not permitted to be alone with a suitor. Courtship was conducted in the presence of the young woman's relatives, "under the blanket." That is, the young man brought a blanket to the young woman's family tipi. Behind this blanket, the couple could converse in whispers, illustrating the modest behaviour that was the traditional cultural standard among Lakota people.

In another example, extramarital affairs among the Lakota were proscribed. In fact, a Lakota woman was not even permitted to touch or braid the hair of another woman's husband if she was not related to the man. Likewise, if a Lakota husband braided another woman's hair, it signalled romantic or sexual intentions, to which his wife would vigorously object.

Women have always been highly esteemed and honoured among Indigenous societies throughout Canada and the United States, many of which are matricentric (such as the Haida in the west; the Lakota-Dakota-Nakoda peoples, the Six Nations Confederacy, and other cultures farther east; and the Cherokee to the south). Modest behaviour among these peoples is characteristic of powerful and well-brought-up women.

In short, the Indian princess or maiden was a construct that worked to validate imagined white, masculine experiences. The Indian princess appears in many forms of popular culture, from Land O' Lakes Butter branding[31] to Disney's *Pocahontas*.[32] As Bird suggests, Pocahontas signified more than just the figure of an Indigenous woman; she was a metaphor for the land itself and was seen as welcoming the white male settler in accordance with colonial imperatives. Whether the woman was sacrificing herself or being sacrificed by riding a canoe over Niagara Falls,[33] by offering up the bounty of nature as a stick of butter, or by her inevitable attraction to non-Native settlers, her role was one of validation for colonization.[34]

In *Selling the Indian*, Erik Trump points out that the image of "squaw drudges" drew a popular nineteenth- and early twentieth-century comparison between civilization and savagery.[35] Usually such characters were depicted as overworked, oversexed, and having too many children, in juxtaposition with "civilized" women. The lyrics of the song "I'm an Indian Too," from the 1940s musical *Annie Get Your Gun*, illustrate this last stereotype: "Looking like a flour sack with two papooses on my back, and three papooses on the way."[36] The song suggests irresponsible over-procreation by Indigenous women, similar to Michel Foucault's description of the social policing of childbirth in relation to problematized sexuality over the past two centuries.[37] The sexuality and reproduction of Indigenous people were scrutinized at the same time that Indigenous women were sexualized as a means of othering and dehumanizing them. Associating self-control with civility and morality was a means of self-definition for the British Empire; this practice was passed on via the American and Canadian puritanical ethos.[38]

Conversely, for white society and its colonies, nineteenth- and twentieth-century social liberal reform institutions such as the public museum and compulsory schools provided technologies for citizens to refine their thoughts and behaviours.[39] Such institutions, housing the objects taken from and sometimes the actual bodies of Indigenous people suggested that the more advanced society had the responsibility to tame and contain savage and exotic bodies by studying and assimilating them through the institutions of civilization.[40] The widely circulated media images and discourses constituting Indigenous identity in the nineteenth and twentieth centuries were indicative of the paternalistic policies and institutions ostensibly aimed at protecting Indigenous people. A starkly negative example was the residential schools discussed in Chapters 1 and 2. However, like popular media, liberal reform institutions such as museums also produced vast archives of paintings, photographs, and films that Indigenous artists now use as a resource in their disruption of colonial assumptions and the erasures they facilitate.

Kent Monkman: Remediating and Amending Canonical Works

While the imaginary Indian has proliferated in popular culture over the past 150 years, European and North American painters over the past two centuries sometimes constituted Indigenous identity by erasing it from their landscapes altogether. European painters, often from highly industrialized areas or pastoral environments with gently rolling hills, were inspired by the dramatic topography of the Americas. They portrayed its lands as an Eden untouched by human hands and ripe for European settlement.[41] Painters who used the same style of realism to depict Indigenous people in the nineteenth and early twentieth centuries more directly reflected a number of cultural beliefs in their works. Some painters, including George Catlin and Paul Kane, sought to document Indigenous peoples and cultures under the assumption that these peoples and cultures were destined for extinction. They captured those images they thought would

Figure 3.1 *Triumph of Mischief*, Kent Monkman, 2007 | *Courtesy of Kent Monkman and the National Gallery of Canada*

look authentic (pre-contact) for their non-Indigenous patrons. Such portraits of Indigenous peoples from throughout the Americas were prolific, and these white male artistic figures became central in the colonial construction of Indigenous identity, in particular reflecting an imperialist nostalgia through the trope of the vanishing Indian.

In response, Kent Monkman, a Canadian artist of Cree ancestry, sees his paintings as "a way of reminding people that the land was inhabited by Indigenous peoples first." In a personal communication, Monkman stated that the omission of Indigenous people in famous landscape paintings was a way of "representing North America as an empty piece of real estate, almost advertising it for development." In some of his most notable paintings, Monkman reproduces famous landscapes and populates them in his own unique way. *The Triumph of Mischief* (2007), part of the 2013 Sakahan Indigenous International Art Exhibition at the National Gallery of Canada, recreates the Albert Bierstadt painting *Looking Up at the Yosemite Valley* (1863–65) and references a number of classical works and characters. A reimagining of history takes place in several parts of the painting. For example, in a humorous turn, Lewis and Clark are being mauled by a bear.[42] George Catlin, Paul Kane, and Edward Curtis also appear in the painting, along with figures from Indigenous and Greek mythologies (see Figure 3.1).

The figures in *The Triumph of Mischief* are mostly male and largely nude. While the painting challenges colonial legacies through remediation, Monkman's work also queers prior media forms by confounding the male/female binary and heteronormative sexuality, which he suggests was imposed on Indigenous people via colonization.[43] Monkman's works are often sexually charged and homoerotic, while confronting the violence of colonization with a sense of humour. Along those lines, in the centre of *The Triumph of Mischief* is the flamboyant, transgendered persona invented by Monkman, Miss

Chief Eagle Testicle. Miss Chief is a berdache, or a "two-spirited" person, someone who resists male/female binaries.[44] According to Monkman, "two-spirited" people existed in Indigenous cultures prior to colonization without facing the same sense of stigma associated with Christian-influenced sexuality.[45] George Catlin's painting *Dance to the Berdache* (1835–37) was the inspiration behind *The Triumph of Mischief*.

Miss Chief's aesthetic resembles that of the singer Cher from the album *Half-Breed*. In performances of the song "Half-Breed," Cher would don a full headdress and sit atop a horse in a skimpy, beaded outfit while belting out the lyrics about the trials of being from a bi-racial (Cherokee/white) background. Cher's look was also an appropriation of that used by Penobscot actress Molly Spotted Elk (1903–77), who starred in such films as H.P. Carver's *The Silent Enemy* (1930) and travelled extensively as a performer. As Monkman points out, Spotted Elk and Cher, like Miss Chief, were pushing male/female binaries by cross-dressing in headdresses, which were traditionally worn by Plains Indian chiefs, who were male. In his *Emergence of a Legend* series, Monkman appropriates the aesthetics of and pays homage to Molly Spotted Elk.

Monkman's work reflects his own creative expression, and his nod to queer culture is a means of critiquing colonization and reversing inequitable relations of power. However, it does not necessarily reflect the cultural traditions of other Indigenous people. While remediated art is an important means of protesting the colonizers' dehumanizing gender stereotypes, there is a (hopefully minimal) risk that, for those who mistake artistic expression as representative, this sort of artistic remediation might further perpetuate the (often sarcastic) stereotypes that Indigenous art parodies.

Remediation takes many forms in Monkman's work. In addition to being an accomplished painter who reproduces canonical landscapes in order to correct their erasure of

Figure 3.2 *Dance to Miss Chief*, Kent Monkman, 2010 | *Courtesy of Kent Monkman*

Indigenous people, Monkman also directs and appears in live performances, photography, and film.

In his music video *Dance to Miss Chief* (the title of which is a reference to Catlin's *Dance to the Berdache*), Monkman includes scenes from a German Karl May western featuring Winnetou, the fictitious, blue-eyed Indian warrior (see Figure 3.2). In the music video, shots of Miss Chief dancing enticingly are intermixed with segments from the western. The shot/reverse shot technique creates the effect of a flirtatious wooing between Winnetou and Miss Chief.[46] Native men drum and dance as they celebrate Miss Chief, as in Catlin's original painting, but the techno beat and Miss Chief's sheer red outfit and high heels clearly set the video in a more contemporary moment. In addition to being a comedic, tongue-in-cheek re-appropriation of the western, *Dance to Miss Chief* pokes fun at the German fascination with American Indians and calls into question the hyper-masculinity of the cinematic character of the noble savage as played by French actor Pierre Brice.

Although the character of Miss Chief certainly has some camp value, for Monkman, it is important to distinguish the character of Miss Chief from conventional forms of drag. While Monkman explained in our personal communication that drag has a "comedic value" and is meant as a form of entertainment in gay bars, Miss Chief appears primarily in films or performance pieces staged at museums where she is responding to specific collections. Examples include her 2007 performance piece *Séance* at the Royal Ontario Museum in Toronto and her 2012 piece *Miss Chief: Justice of the Piece*, performed at the National Museum of the American Indian in Washington, DC.

Similarly, in the 2007 film *Shooting Geronimo*, Monkman confronts filmic practices by white filmmakers such as Edward Curtis, who worked hard to contrive images that would look "authentic" for mostly non-Native audiences (see Figure 3.3). While Curtis's photos and films were thought of as documentary, the filmmaker attempted to achieve a pre-contact aesthetic by removing objects that looked too Western, and he required his Native models and actors to wear costumes that his audiences would perceive as traditional.

In *Shooting Geronimo*, Monkman recreates the aesthetics of a silent movie from the turn of the century by using black-and-white film, scoring the film with old-time-sounding piano music, and narrating it with intertitles (title cards). He includes an Edward Curtis–like character, Frederick Curtis, who is attempting to direct two Indigenous characters, Johnny Silvercloud and Blake Tenderfoot from the fictitious films *The Red Menace* and *Ghost Dance of the American Indian*. Curtis's films are references to countless westerns depicting the ignoble, bloodthirsty savage on the war path, as well as early salvage films, which sought to record Indian cultural practices, such as Thomas Edison's *Sioux Ghost Dance* (1894).

The idea of film as a documentary medium is called into question in humorous moments of *Shooting Geronimo*, when Curtis asks the grinning Silvercloud, who does not look

Figure 3.3 Still from *Shooting Geronimo*, Kent Monkman, 2007 | *Courtesy of Kent Monkman*

tough at all, to look more like a "fierce renegade" as he is playing Geronimo. When he asks both actors to perform "authentic" Native dances, they take a cue from Miss Chief and perform break-dancing moves. The actors also struggle with the costumes and long wigs provided by the director. While Silvercloud over-acts and flips his wig dramatically, Tenderfoot looks uncomfortable, getting his hair stuck in his mouth. In this film, as with many of her appearances, Miss

Chief acts as a trickster character, or a mischievous figure who creates disruptions, which are often humorous. In this case, she is an intervening force, who resists linear time (with her introduction of break-dancing into this turn-of-the-century scene) and throws a hitch in Curtis's plans.

Although working to denaturalize a long tradition of playing Indian in Hollywood, Miss Chief herself participates in redfacing by using some of the same signifiers to indicate Indian-ness, including, for example, her use of a Plains Indian headdress. Michelle Raheja describes redfacing as "a complex practice that was at times transgressive but reified negative stereotypes at others."[47] As Raheja suggests, there were a number of reasons Indigenous people engaged in "performances of the 'Indian,'" including economic opportunities and escape from poverty.[48] Similarly, in response to the question whether a difference exists between Indigenous performance of redface and non-Indigenous performance of redface, Monkman stated in our personal communication, "Of course there is [a difference]. Artists like myself are making a profound political statement about basically attempted extermination of our people."

While he employs painting and film to respond to pervasive constructions of Indigenous people by white artists and filmmakers, Monkman also sees the museum as an important site of intervention and self-referential critique. He states:

A lot of my work deals with challenging the work that was done by artists in the nineteenth century, so basically their works are still represented at the museum and put forward, and the authority of their work is still forwarded by current museum practice. So it's very important that I also engage with museums because they are the ones who are perpetuating some of the same ideas that were originally held by those artists. Occasionally there's room to engage in a dialogue with those original works, to open the conversation and to challenge the subjectivity of some of the original artists.

He continues,

Museums are repositories of all kinds of objects from the past through to the present, so they have enormous value and interest for me just in terms of finding works in the collection to … find inspiration from … to create response works linked to certain pieces, or to find connecting themes that link entire bodies of work from different artists. The main thing is really that they continue to present these works without any challenge to their original intent. That's what I've found through a number of different museum projects, was that these works by Paul Kane or George Catlin were still presented as voices of authority on Indigenous people … I think some work is being done to unpack that and to shed light on the past contrivance of artists from that period so that their work is presented with some kind of critical light shed on it as well. But still, more often than not, it's easier for them to hang the work without contextualizing it.

Monkman's critiques about the uncritical treatment of canonical artists, including Paul Kane, ring true in the Royal Ontario Museum's Daphne Cockwell Gallery of Canada: First Peoples. Paul Kane's oil paintings of Indigenous life in North America, created in a studio based on his field sketches and imagination, are positioned prominently and hung with very little commentary. It is up to the visitor to generate critical insights that challenge the authority of Kane's works. The gallery is more successful when contemporary artists are invited to engage such works in conversation with Indigenous points out, Indigenous reporters face challenges too, and realistically will likely continue to make up a small minority in the newsroom: "There are some non-Aboriginal reporters who do a fantastic job covering Aboriginal communities ... being Indigenous may be helpful in the first five minutes. But after that, it's just about good solid journalism and good storytelling."

Among the challenges that all reporters face, regardless of their background, McCue notes "the daily deadline" and the costs of in-depth reports. News media are primarily centred in urban areas, making it difficult to cover stories in remote locations. Time and geography are major constraints faced by all journalists, and battles about time and resource allocation also need to be fought at the level of the senior producer. As McCue explains, while all newsrooms face such challenges,

> it becomes more of an issue when you're working in an Indigenous community because there is a real difference, a cultural understanding, about time. A lot of Indigenous people don't necessarily operate ... with a watch or your average twelve-hour clock in mind. They are operating on "Indian Time," which is a very cultural notion, doing things in a good way, in a right way and as long as it takes to do things in that way. Operating on that notion of time must ensure that proper respect is included in whatever process in which you're included. None of those things are newsroom deadline time. And so that is always a real battle for any journalist whether they are Indigenous or not ...
>
> When there is a story that's breaking, people want to know what's going on and our audiences want to know, have answers, and we have a duty to give them those answers. But, at the same time we can give them those answers in some kind of way that also allows us to look at the

story longer and in more depth that will come away with more context rather than just parachuting in and getting really unsatisfactory cursory looks at these communities.

At the same time that journalists may struggle to balance the priorities of the newsroom and those of Indigenous communities, they may not know which stories matter to the Indigenous communities. For example, McCue notes the Idle No More movement as one of many examples of stories that mainstream journalists reported too late – long after Indigenous people had recognized it as significant. Similarly, violence against Indigenous women and the large numbers of Indigenous women who have been murdered and gone missing in Canada in recent years have been important concerns to Indigenous communities for many years but were long overlooked in mainstream reporting.[29]

Mainstream Coverage and Indigenous Media: The Benefits of a Wide Audience

Given the long history of problems with mainstream coverage, we wondered why McCue was not drawn to work for news outlets that cater more to Indigenous interests. There is a long history of Indigenous journalism in Canada. Indigenous print media (newsletters, newspapers, and magazines) have been active, often due to the efforts of staff who support publications even when they are underfunded, through paid subscriptions, advertising, or government subsidies.[30] Also, remote communities have been at the forefront worldwide of broadcast and film by and for Indigenous people, which has extended into new media productions.[31] A notable example is *APTN National News* on the Aboriginal Peoples Television Network (APTN). APTN presents a departure from the usual news formats by privileging Indigenous perspectives and audiences. APTN has been described by media studies scholar Sigurjon Baldur Hafsteinsson as a form of "deep democracy" that is "already transgressive in that it gives voice to groups that assert their sovereignty within the boundaries of Canada."[32]

APTN and *APTN National News* came out of the advocacy and coordination of broadcasters through the Northern Native Broadcast Access Program, which eventually formed the network's predecessor, the satellite-based Television Northern Canada (TVNC).[33] Launched in 1999, APTN has been heralded internationally as a model for independent Indigenous broadcasting, and *APTN National News* has been lauded for its informed coverage of national Indigenous concerns.[34] As media policy scholar Marian Bredin notes, "Before the creation of APTN, there was no national outlet for Aboriginal television in Canada and relatively little incentive for mainstream networks to acquire or develop information or entertainment programming that reflected the nation's Indigenous peoples."[35] Moreover, as Bredin points out, APTN has supported and triggered the creation of production companies that focus on Indigenous content.[36]

Despite the good work of Indigenous news outlets such as APTN, mainstream news remains an important medium for reporting issues that impact the lives of Indigenous people. Mainstream news audiences continue to be composed of both Indigenous and non-Indigenous people.[37] McCue notes the wide reach and audience that attracted him to CBC. He states, "On a nightly basis on *The National*, we get a million viewers on average. And there is nowhere else in the country ... in TV, other than *CTV News*, where I can reach that number of people." He continues:

I get a little bit of a rush, to be honest with you, when I report a story, and it provokes conversation ... and another story and another story ... That's part of what I'm here to do, and so working in the mainstream was the best way for me to get the broadest possible audience. The other benefit is to have access to a great deal of resources.

Don't get me wrong, I have had ups and downs, peaks and valleys working with the CBC over the years, in particular over Aboriginal coverage. There have been times when I have wanted to shift over to APTN and wondered what it would be like to be telling stories just to an Indigenous audience.[38] I hope that maybe sometime in my career I'll be able to do that. But for the most part, the CBC has treated me pretty well and given me lots of opportunities to tell the kinds of stories that I want to tell. As long as that relationship continues, then I'm a pretty happy guy ...

But, God knows I'm the biggest flag-waving supporter of APTN and Indigenous media. It is incredibly important that we are setting the agenda. I loved the ad campaign a couple years back that if APTN was there, history would have been told differently. That should be the rallying cry for all Indigenous media around the country. But that said, there is a real role – and I keep hearing this from people – for having Indigenous folks in the mainstream media as well. We can't just play in our own sandbox.

We live in a country where, going back to that *Delgamuukw* decision, the famous last line is "We are all here to stay."[39] And so, we need to continue that conversation with Canadians about our place here, who we are, and what our hopes and dreams and fears are.

If we aren't speaking in forums that they pay attention to, then they won't know. And they won't know when people are making decisions that impact our lives and aspirations as Indigenous people, without ever knowing what it is that we hope to do. Which is why I do think that we need to have folks in the mainstream.

While McCue notes the importance of exposing a wider, non-Indigenous audience to the concerns of Indigenous people, some of his mainstream news coverage is similar to that of *APTN National News*. As we discuss below in our description of McCue's story on Marlene Bird, McCue includes interviews with Indigenous informants who take their time, and he doesn't reduce their words into sound bites. He also provides foregrounding of Indigenous issues that is atypical of mainstream coverage. As anthropologist Kristin Dowell argues in *Sovereign Screens*, "Cultural protocol is reflected on-screen by not interrupting elders in the editing process, often resulting in longer 'talking head' shots than would be acceptable in mainstream media."[40] Such context is essential considering the legacy of reporting that has delegitimized and erased Indigenous people and perspectives.

Violence against Indigenous Women: Marlene Bird's Story
Through their demands for a national inquest, Indigenous movements and organizations such as Sisters in Spirit, Native Women's Association of Canada, Idle No More, and the Truth and Reconciliation Commission have brought widespread attention to Canada's murdered and missing Indigenous women. However, Indigenous communities have long been aware of the violence faced by their mothers, aunties, sisters, daughters, cousins, and friends.[41] Such violence is part and parcel of a misogynist colonial system. For the most part, press attention on the violence has until recently been "relatively minimal."[42] The Native Women's Association of Canada has gathered data on the Aboriginal women who have been murdered or gone missing; as of 2010, more than half the cases remained unsolved.[43] The government of Canada estimates that more than 1,200 Indigenous women have been murdered or gone missing in recent years, but Indigenous Affairs Minister Carolyn Bennett commented in

2016 that the problem was likely "way bigger" than originally anticipated.[44] Scholars suggest that the omission of violence against Indigenous women in the news media has been
related to the low social value placed on Indigenous women
in Canada. While Hollywood cinema has tended to reproduce the stereotype of the sexualized Indian princess, com-
munications scholars Yasmin Jiwani and Mary Lynn Young
argue that news coverage in Canada paints a similarly stereotypical but much less sympathetic picture of Indigenous
women. In a seven-year study of *Globe and Mail* news coverage related to Indigenous women, the researchers said the
newspaper often relied on the "fallen woman" stereotype by
focusing on stories about conflict, violence, custody battles,
drug addiction, prostitution, and poverty.[45]

Similarly, media analyst Kristen Gilchrist argues that although murdered and missing Indigenous women in Canada
come from "all walks of life," their treatment as "unworthy
victims" might be one of the reasons they have received much
less sympathetic coverage than white victims. Her study exam-
ines news coverage about six women who went missing or
were found murdered during a similar time period. Three of
the women were Aboriginal and three were not. The stories
about the women from mainstream culture received more
sympathetic, prolific, and prominent coverage.[46]

In considering the scant coverage of Indigenous gender
violence in the past, it is worth drawing a comparison with
Duncan McCue's more nuanced and prominent coverage in
January 2015 on *The National*: "Marlene Bird: Aboriginal
Woman's Story of Struggle and Survival." The broadcast
story, which focused on one particular case, was part of a
larger feature discussing violence and Indigenous women
more generally. Written components and video clips were
also posted on the CBC website.[47] Marlene Bird is a Cree
woman who was brutally attacked by three people in June
2014. She was beaten, sexually assaulted, set on fire, and left

for dead in a parking lot in Prince Albert, Saskatchewan. She survived the attack, but lost both her legs and the use of one of her eyes. McCue's story recounts Bird's abuse-ridden life and her continuing struggles to get off the street.

According to the story, Bird had alcoholic parents, was abused in residential school as a young girl, and faced severe physical violence at the hands of a former boyfriend. She began using alcohol at an early age and continued drinking after she became a parent. In response, authorities removed her children from her care. Finally, McCue's story chronicled her life on the street as an alcoholic.

Bird's horrible circumstances exemplify some of the worst aspects of Indigenous experiences in Canada today. McCue takes the time, through extensive interviews over the span of nineteen minutes, to humanize Bird and her current partner, Patrick Lavallee, a recovering alcoholic. He notes the support that Lavallee has continued to exhibit in his attempts to care for Bird, despite the harsh conditions faced by both because of their lack of permanent housing and Bird's double amputation. Lavallee stopped drinking and remained clean and sober for many months in order to care for Bird. McCue characterizes their experience as an unlikely but powerful "love story" (see Figure 5.2).

McCue is patient with those providing comments; the story moves at a slow pace and includes long interview excerpts. The comments from Bird and her partner are unpolished, and the couple is far from media-savvy, but their perspectives are legitimized and treated as valuable. McCue also employs drawings by graphic-novel artist Dan Archer to illustrate and re-enact portions of the story. These are particularly effective, for example, in depicting Bird's earlier experiences as a young woman in residential school.

Although McCue must work within the confines of the news cycle form and structure, he is respectful to the participants and moves beyond their disabilities, alcoholism, and

Figure 5.2 Image from Duncan McCue's "Marlene Bird: Aboriginal Woman's Story of Struggle and Survival" | *Courtesy of CBC*

victimhood to provide a more nuanced portrait of their conditions, even the ways in which they have managed to maintain a humble sense of humour. Importantly, the story more broadly addresses the alarming rates of violence against Indigenous women in Canada, where Indigenous women bear the brunt of a general societal antipathy towards Indigenous people. While the brutality of Bird's story has likely shocked viewers, McCue and the CBC have thematized it to make it clear that her experiences are far from unique. As the story illustrates, the violence faced by Bird is endemic to Indigenous communities and is part of a longer colonial legacy. In her interview, Bird asks, "Why did he do this to me? Why would he do that to a woman? That's where you come from, a woman. Why would he want to try to kill me?" Although she asks it simply and gently, her question is potent and reverberates, as the answer lies not just with the perpetrators of the crime but in the logics of an oppressive colonial regime.

❀ ❀ ❀

Despite the limitations of mainstream media in covering Indigenous issues, Duncan McCue's presence is encouraging as he can push agenda-setters to pay attention to issues that matter to Indigenous people. Moreover, he can model journalistic practices based on respect and relationality with Indigenous communities as he trains a new generation of news professionals to do the same. As a journalist, McCue opens up opportunities for storytelling that re-orients mainstream concerns to include Indigenous perspectives. He models storytelling that privileges Indigenous people, even when the subjects of his stories are not aware of media conventions and do not fit reductive identity constructs. McCue's message is clear to people who are contemplating a career in mainstream journalism covering Indigenous affairs, regardless of whether they are Indigenous:

> I'd tell them what a rewarding career I have had. I'd tell them how blessed I have been to be in the homes of Aboriginal people who have opened up their doors to tell their stories to me about all kinds of things ... about hunting buffalo; about diabetes; about suicide; about how upset they were about eagles being poached; about how to make a drum; about their child being taken away from them by child welfare; stories about rock music and disco and how fun it is to make that kind of music. I could just keep on going for another half an hour about the privilege of having those stories shared with me and then to be entrusted with telling those stories to other people. I mean, that is just such an honour and such a blessing.
>
> What advice would I give? It is such a rewarding line of work for any reporter. And I've talked with many senior news reporters in Canada who will say that some of the most memorable stories that they have worked on have been in Indigenous communities because some of these stories just aren't heard by Canadians and so, it

goes back to Dickens' line (he was a storyteller from another culture, you know), "It's the best of times and the worst of times."

There are great heartaches in my efforts to tell some of those stories. There have been days where I've torn my hair out saying, "Why am I doing this?" But that's all part and parcel of what ultimately has just been an absolute privilege to be able to tell stories in Indian country. Any reporter, Indigenous or non-Indigenous person, who makes a serious effort to try to tell and share some of the stories of First Nations people in this country with the rest of Canada is going to have those really positive and sometimes really negative experiences ...

I stand up and do my on-camera and some director talks into my ear: "OK, Duncan you're on." And then I talk and then it goes off into the ether. And I don't sit with people as they watch television. I don't know that they're necessarily having conversations about what I just did. But I do hope that somehow stories can change something, can make a difference in changing the dialogue in this country. To quote Thomas King, "Stories are all we are."

Conclusion
Media Tactics Old and New

The past shall be made dynamic by the demands
of the present and the hopes of the future.

– Audra Simpson, *Mohawk Interruptus*

We highlighted media interventions in Canadian culture to illustrate the profound adaptability of Indigenous agents who employ tactical manoeuvres within the structures of power. Throughout this book, we have focused on sites where understandings of Indigenous people are shaped for wide audiences and where media and media forms are subverted for Indigenous purposes. These include a national truth commission and associated archives, an online television portal, art and film institutions, and national news outlets. While they are disparate sites, each illustrates the creative use of media to highlight some of the most fundamental concerns held by Indigenous people today. While the institutions discussed in this book may be limited by cultural form, ownership, and control, they can be harnessed in sometimes surprising ways as mechanisms for denaturalizing the very power structures out of which they emerged.

While the media interventions highlighted in this book do not propose radical breaks, and the Indigenous actors may not captain the larger institutions in which they intervene, their use of media tactics is about cultural resurgence and survival, which demands creative play where circumstances are far from ideal. As Alanis Obomsawin reminds us in the opening paragraphs of this book, while Indigenous people may not always control the structures that affect them, there are still opportunities for them to assert their agency.

The discussions in this book highlight the creative negotiations, or tactics, that Indigenous actors employ to navigate their complex, contemporary experiences. The institutions in which they intervene may not be designed to benefit their interests, but media tactics provide opportunities for the disruption of the typical flows of history, discourse, and image. The radical break that some Indigenous thinkers have prescribed[1] may indeed foster Indigenous ways of being and knowing, but the examples herein illustrate a manoeuvring within a colonial system in which the actors negotiate a necessary relationship with the larger culture, for better or worse.

We are interested in the ways in which Indigenous actors "manage the present" through not just an acceptance of contemporary paradigms but also an elaborate dance with them.[2] The simultaneous engagement with and rejection of settler-colonial models within these media interventions is a testament to the profound dynamism of the Indigenous people we have discussed. We looked to media tactics that reflect elaborate negotiations that both accept and refuse the terms of contemporary mediated and politicized landscapes. We approached media as always socially and culturally situated.

As the sites we explored were diverse, we adapted our conceptual, theoretical, and methodological frameworks as necessary. For example, Indigenous identity as an umbrella category was both employed and contested. In some cases, we illustrated articulations of broad Indigenous experiences with some oscillation between specificity and more universal themes, as with the Inuit residential school survivor testimonials discussed in Chapter 2. In most of the cases and institutions we discussed, however, appeals to broad articulations of Indigeneity were emphasized as a means of mobilizing wide concerns.

The perspectives of our Indigenous participants were central, and their stories formed a web out of which the rest of the book grew. We invited Indigenous elders, artists, filmmakers and festival organizers, Truth and Reconciliation Commission representatives, activists, reporters, and journalism educators to speak with us. The people with whom we spoke were generous with their time and insights, well beyond our expectations. We hope we have done their stories justice; we understand the stakes are serious in recording these stories for future generations. In moments where we employed participant observation, we were inspired by what we saw. The joy and warmth exhibited when Indigenous artists gathered at places such as the imagineNATIVE Film + Media Arts Festival in Toronto reminded us of the importance of community, culture, relationality, and hope. It also illustrated the intensely social nature of Indigenous media making.

Through the heartbreaking testimonials and tears at Truth and Reconciliation Commission gatherings, we could feel the determination that residential school survivors had when sharing their stories, and their hopes for safeguarding future generations of Indigenous children from enduring the pain and suffering they had experienced. The strength that survivors and intergenerational survivors exhibited in discussing the worst moments of their lives was intensely humbling.

Rather than assuming the position of detached scientific observers, we found it was only appropriate to act with respect, assuming a kind of "ethnographic refusal" in which we shared the concerns of the people with whom we spent time and who gifted us with their stories.[3] Even so, there were several cases in which the irony of our position as academics attempting to do ethical work in Indigenous studies was stark. For example, before a discussion with Alanis Obomsawin about her film *Trick or Treaty*, which is in part about how the Crown dispossessed Indigenous people of their lands and rights by coaxing and coercing them into signing treaties, we asked the filmmaking legend to sign a consent form. The form is in place to ensure participants' rights (and Alanis Obomsawin is a seasoned professional who has likely seen many of these), but it also acts as a reminder of how the institution wields power over the discussion through its own legal protection. While we adapted our approach according to circumstances, it was not a seamless process as we also worked within institutional confines.

The topics we examined also reinforced the need for a dynamic theoretical approach. We found that Indigenous responses within power relations cannot be reduced to over-determined frameworks. We also described models for understanding Indigenous texts that do not cling to strict aesthetic topologies, further demonstrating the dynamic characteristics of current Indigenous media practices. For example, the imagineNATIVE film festival includes works based on the identity of the filmmaker and a well-established web of social connections. It models how we might rethink Indigenous media and support Indigenous filmmakers without adhering to an aesthetic definition.

Our explorations into Indigenous identity and social connections in relation to media tactics have also shown us that we do not need to abandon cultural meanings in favour of reductive theoretical models. As the examples throughout this book illustrate, media practices have particular meanings in Indigenous communities, which makes a cultural approach to media studies all the more necessary.[4] For example, by privileging concerns about class, we miss the unique Indigenous experiences of displacement and territorial dispossession, which simultaneously attacks place-based cultures and mobilization based on identity.[5] At the same time, post-structuralist accounts on their own do not adequately explore the negotiations through which Indigenous people engage with power relations on the ground. In summary, while the frameworks of mainstream (Marxist and post-structuralist) theorists are useful, theory is best employed when adapted for the specific modern conditions of Indigenous people, their own ideas, and the histories that have shaped them.

We have reviewed just a small number of Indigenous interventions into the newer culture's consciousness and into Indigenous communities in Canada. We have attempted to highlight not just the positive work but also the problems that persist. For example, as the Truth and Reconciliation Commission (TRC) pointed out in its final report summary, one of the most essential concerns to Indigenous communities across Canada today is the alarmingly high numbers of Indigenous women who have been murdered or gone missing in recent years.[6] Indeed, pervasive violence against Indigenous women is a theme that emerges in one way or another in every chapter of this book. While mainstream institutions (legal, social, cultural) have clearly failed Indigenous women, the TRC's invocation for a national inquiry into those who have been murdered and gone missing is reinforced by thousands of mediated testimonials recounting the abhorrent violence that Indigenous people have faced and the continuing legacies of this violence. Indigenous filmmakers, artists, and activists are anchoring this issue in public consciousness. Indigenous agents are demanding that institutions be accountable for their complacency and participation in the erasures that have happened in the past and that continue to occur.

As we write, the TRC has disbanded, and the National Centre for Truth and Reconciliation (NCTR) is organizing a digital archive that will be available to the Canadian public. It includes the statements gathered in the North through the

Inuit sub-commission. NCTR leaders are challenging a court decision requiring the destruction of nearly forty thousand residential school survivor statements gathered through the Independent Assessment Process.[7] Indigenous artists across the country continue their work critiquing the structures of power that disadvantage their people. At the same time, imagineNATIVE is gearing up for another festival that will attract mainstream and Indigenous audiences and filmmakers from around the world. Duncan McCue is training the next generation of news professionals to cover Indigenous issues with respect and relationality.

Indigenous elders, traditional leaders, and knowledge keepers such as Alanis Obomsawin are inspiring the next generation of Indigenous youth to lead their people and have identified a powerful cultural resurgence underway. Many young people are using social and mainstream media to challenge power structures and to promote the goals of cultural resurgence. For example, Anishinaabe comedian Ryan McMahon uses hard-hitting humour to denaturalize settler-colonial thinking in his performances and online podcasts, including *Stories from the Land* and *Red Man Laughing*. Tsilhqot'in storyteller Lisa Charleyboy hosts the national CBC show *New Fire*, which highlights Indigenous youth such as Facebook sensation Savannah "Savvy" Simon. Simon uses the social-networking platform to forward the practice of Mi'kmaq language and sends encouraging messages to young Indigenous people (see Figure 6.1).[8]

Indigenous youth have been handed a difficult and at times overwhelming responsibility to heal and support their communities, but their continuing work through new media is encouraging. Undoubtedly, Indigenous leaders will continue to push Canadian institutions to take Indigenous perspectives seriously, and Indigenous youth will carry on the fight. The mainstream and political powers may never fully acknowledge or understand Indigenous concerns, but